ME AND MY MASK

Cadmus Publishing
www.cadmuspublishing.com

James Melvin Ferebee

Copyright © 2022 James Melvin Ferebee

Published by Cadmus Publishing
www.cadmuspublishing.com
Port Angeles, WA

ISBN: 978-1-63751-134-3

All rights reserved. Copyright under Berne Copyright Convention, Universal Copyright Convention, and Pan-American Copyright Convention. No part of this book may be reproduced, stored in a retrieval system, or transmitted in any form, or by any means, electronic, mechanical, photocopying, recording or otherwise, without prior permission of the author.

This is a work of fiction; therefore, names, characters, places, and incidents are the products of the author's imagination or are used fictitiously. Any resemblance to actual events, locales, or persons, living or dead, is entirely coincidental.

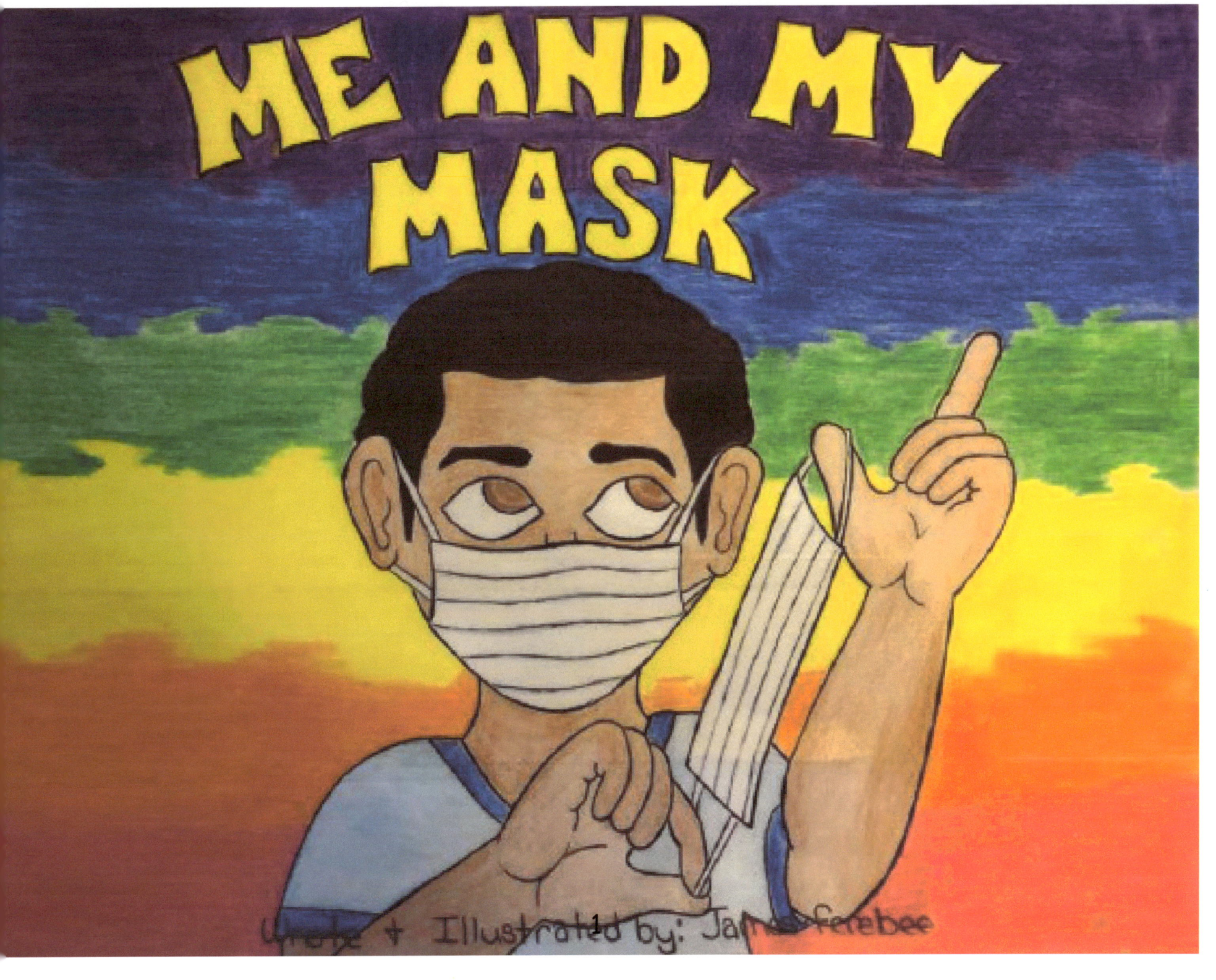

My mommy wears her mask all day long while doing her task. So I ask, "Why is a mask so great?"

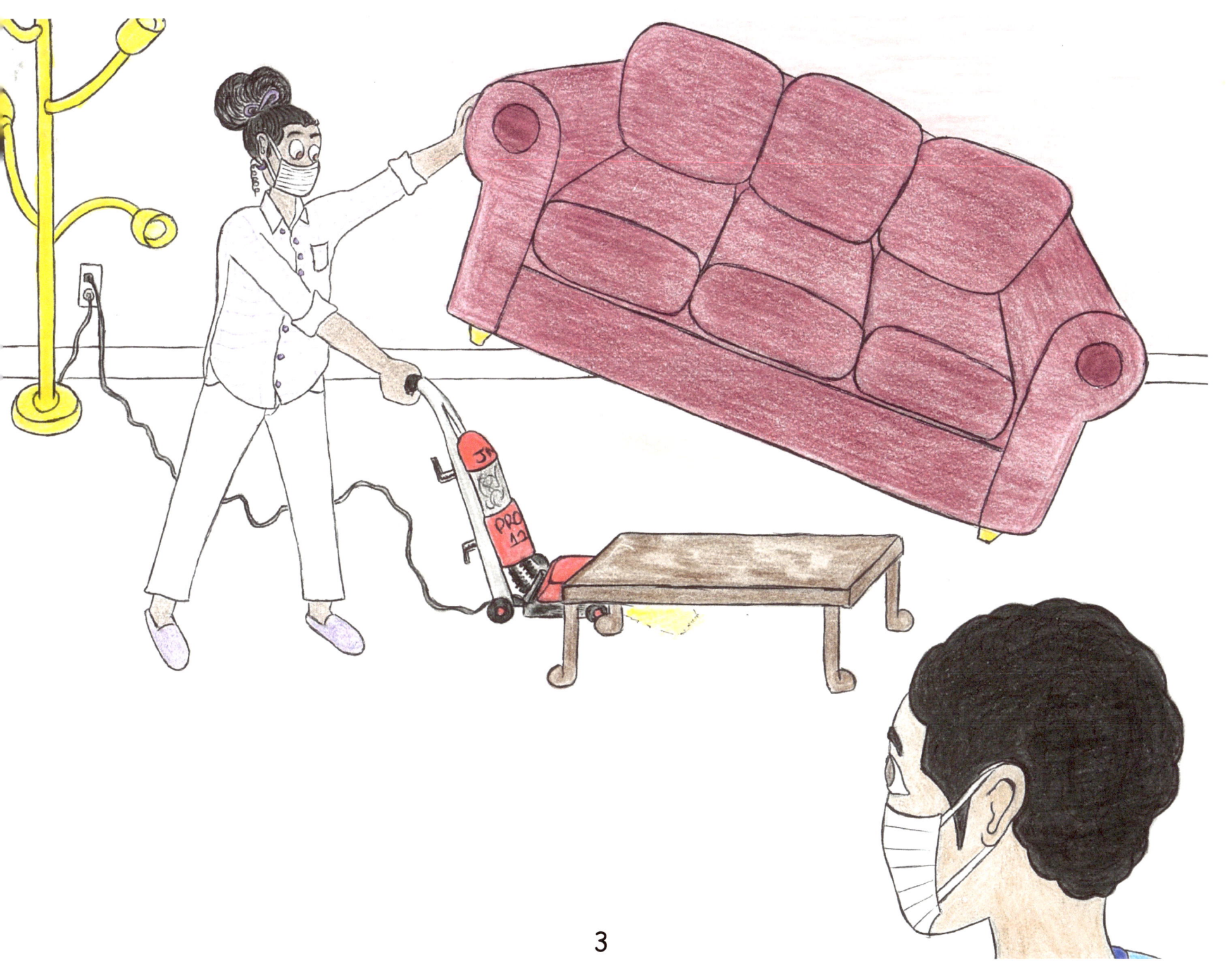

It's itchy, hot, and it hides my face!

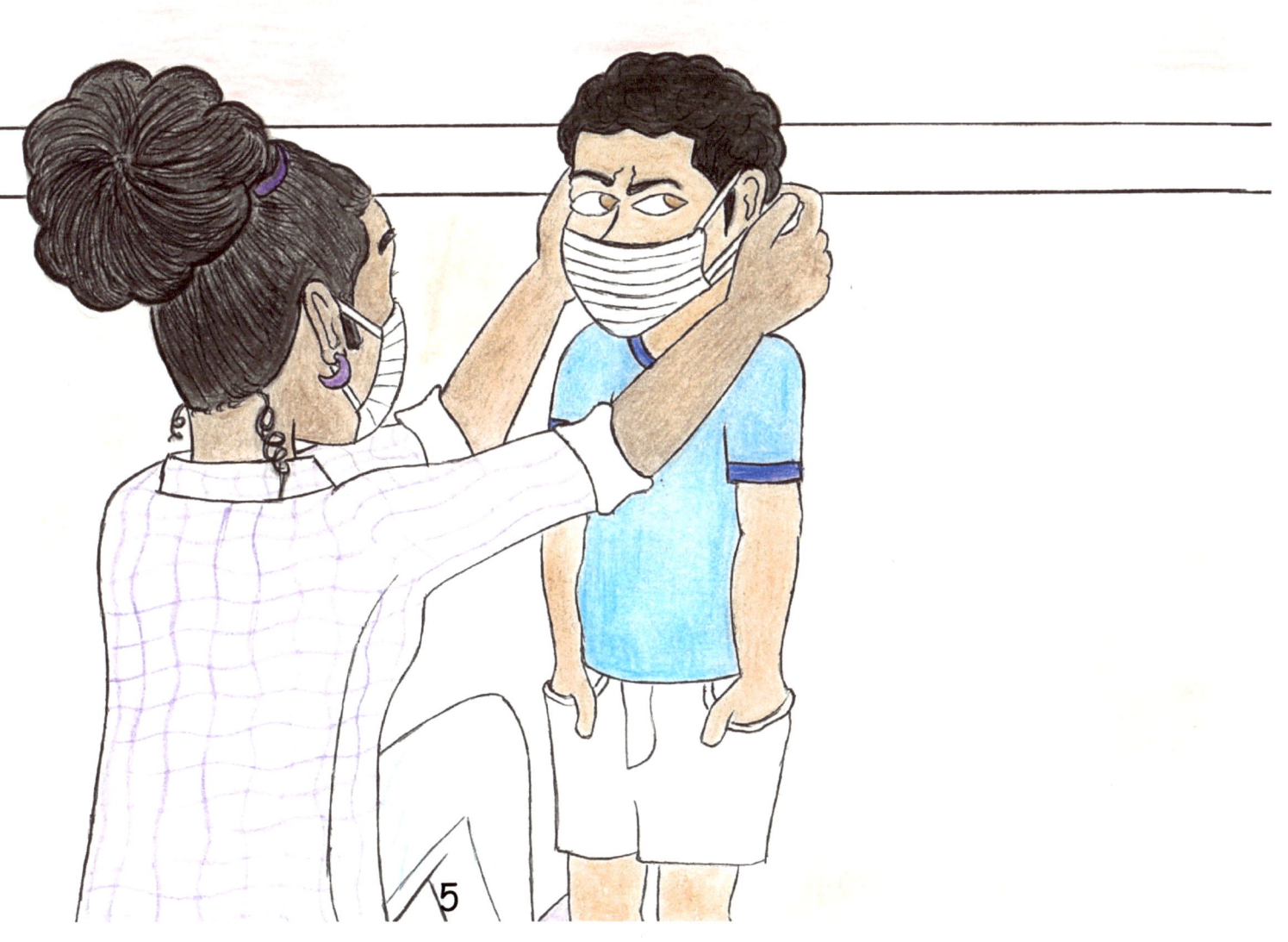

I used to love it when Mommy would kiss me on the cheek. Muah!

No kisses for me as days turn into weeks!

I love pizza, ice cream, and all kinds of sweets!

And this mask gets in between me and the good things that I love to eat!

I even have on my mask when I'm outside playing.

"Don't forget your mask!"
Mommy is always saying!

The dog and I have to play hide-and-seek.

It's because I have no friends allowed around to play hide-and-seek with me.

Mommy says, "We have to start practicing social distancing."

"Can my friends come over now that I am practicing soap and dishes in the sink?"

"Wake up, son! Guess what Mommy has?"
"Oh boy, it's a gift, maybe a toy!"

There's no telling what Mommy may have. Mommy just gave me...

"Another face mask? This can't be a gift. I don't want anything else covering my lips!"

"What's wrong?" Mommy asked. "Don't you like your mask? It has smiley faces. It should make you glad."

"It should have frown faces all over it. This whole mask thing, I just don't get!"

"Masks are good, they are not bad!
Here's why we all should love our mask!

Your mask is a friend that can keep you safe! Masks block most of the germs that can land on your face!

These germs are bad! They will make you sick! But remember, you can't see germs playing their tiny tricks! Germs spread quickly - yes, they move fast.

But not fast enough to not get caught by your mask!"

"Mommy, wow, now I understand! I wear my mask so I don't have to wash my hands! Just kidding, Mommy!"

I sure am glad that I had to ask! So until germs are gone, you'll see.

The End

www.ingramcontent.com/pod-product-compliance
Lightning Source LLC
Chambersburg PA
CBHW041150070526
44583CB00004B/137